We 'til Death Do Part

加藤

Poems by Matt Cooper

Kansas City　Spartan Press　Missouri

Spartan Press
Kansas City, Missouri
spartanpress.com

Copyright © Matt Cooper, 2021
First Edition: 1 3 5 7 9 10 8 6 4 2
ISBN: 978-1-952411-42-7
LCCN: 2020952980

Cover and author photo: Matt Cooper
All rights reserved. No part of this publication may be reproduced or transmitted in any form or by any means, electronic or mechanical, including photocopying, recording or by info retrieval system, without prior written permission from the author.

Special thanks to Jason Ryberg, Shaune Larder, Jeff Guy, Breck and Emily Adkins, Kevin Rabas, Chance Swaim, Albert Goldbarth, Richard Davies, Freyja Hooley, Michael Poage, Linzi Garcia, Matthew Zardoz, Diane Wahto, Milla Mustonen, Brent, Jessica, and Neil Buckley, Vincent Triana, Danny Echo, Dave Massey, Jeff Tymony, Amy Chastain, Jamie and Rob Klem, Clay Calhoun, John and Richard Jones, Matsuri Sakai, Suzuna Abo, Abu Diabo, Alex Skipton, Kondwani Mwale, Avery Chong, Oak Ward, Jerry and Candace Landers, Valerie Haring, Kendall Crocombe, Clayton Walter, Addison Mclaughlin, Chris Wheatley, Scotty Edwards, The Hot Apostles, Daniel Davis, John Patton, Jyuugo Katō as well as Bread Nugent.

And finally thank you to Kaori Katō and Alicia Newell, my spirit parents who guide me in everything I do. We may walk the earth far from one another some days, but in the moments that try our hearts most, we bind in that Gordian sense that is ineffably immune to all the maelstroms and pike wielding ruffians that would conquer and divide us.

You have my fealty to the end.

M.C.
2021

TABLE OF CONTENTS

The Elastic Band of Time / 1
A Fat Little Joke / 3
Something to Utter for Fun / 5
Eyes Closed, then Open / 6
November Breaths / 8
Your Last Words / 9
Knowing the Difference / 11
Reality Shrugs Its Shoulders / 12
Sense For No One But You / 14
Your Reincarnation in a Tanka / 16
Something Novel / 17
Words For a Boy / 18
Fixing Things Means Freedom / 20
A Signal / 21
Existence of Robinson Jeffers / 23
Laughing Over Sake / 24
God Help the World / 25
The Minor League / 27
A Further Maxim / 28
Waka on Hui Neng / 29
Day 1: My Friend The Dying Mouse / 30
Day 2: Your Death, Resurrection, and the
   Key Lime / 31
Day 3: Your Life Returned and I Misunderstood / 33
Ways to Find Her Again / 35
And the Weather / 37
Just the Next One / 39
Happy New Year Calendar Prayer / 41
No Consideration Necessary / 43

A Text Message For Kate / 44
The Game Unto Work / 47
A Photo of Me Psychoanalyzed / 48
A Kind of Popular Thought / 51
A Sense of the Wild / 52
A Nostalgic Treatment / 53
A Working Lesson / 54
A Librarian's Advice / 56
A Man Like an Arrow / 57
A Bit of Time By God / 59
Your Thoughts on me Staring / 60
The Treaty Table / 62
Birth in Terms of a CPU / 63
Apology to All My Broken Watches
   From Childhood / 64
My Pulpit as It Is Now / 66
And Grand Dad Collected Used Golf Balls / 67
Bibles and Messages / 68
With the Wisdom of a Dog / 69
No Tracing the Lines Now / 71
Among the Other Customers / 72
Considering the Alternate Drugs / 74
Advice to My Talkative Peer / 75
A Note on The Fragility of Artistic Minds / 77
A Varying Influence / 79
A Study of You in Ink / 80
A Moment after Your Slut Funeral / 81
In Traffic Court Imagining My Parents
   Were There / 82

To Hear the Sermon / 83
A Monument for Her / 84
A Wrong Choice of Words / 86
No War Today, Just Burnt Food and
   Too Many Spices / 88
Something Small / 90
What You Are Now / 92
Waters in Your Tone / 93
In Response to the Season Change / 94
Tawagoto # 7 / 95
A Humble Question / 96
Emerging Aspirant / 97
From a Spartan / 100
On a Friend's Life / 101
Jackasses / 102
Taking up Residence / 103
Me Ignoring Doctors and Priests Again / 105
A Birthday in Seoul / 106
What Saved Me / 118
Your Performance / 119
Hoping You Will Hear / 122

To the future of a small, bright, precocious boy named Emiliano Sanne Pedro De Leon. This book is for you. You are the one who maketh my spirit to shine.

And For those that couldn't be here for this leg of the trip:
…Leo Tracy Cooper
…Alexander Michael Buckley
…Michael Cissell
And
…Star Hansen
These poems are for you
Wherever you all are.

I'm the last speaker of my language.
As are you, of yours. So many words for this
one thing!—As many as people.

- Albert Goldbarth in *Everyday People*

The Elastic Band of Time

I am starving this morning
As you were for a lifetime after
What my people, my side of
The world chose to leave for you, taking it all with a smile.
And I feel lucky, not because
I've outlasted anyone, but
As a result of undiscerning guidance
From my roaming compatriots who dance the same way
    to storms as I do.
From my peers and teachers and the wobbling
Guitar men whom I worship as they hoof it bleeding
    down Broadway
And to the foster parents who took me in once
On the archipelago where my eyes flashed open
When the entropy of my solipsistic mind
Told me there was nothing in front of my eyes.
It, this life, the short blink of it might have been
Nothing were it not for the moments of
Consideration that this all might be a dream
Where the contents of books make
Up everything we feel and touch and lose and love.
Yet all I could do was praise the
Remains of my blood relatives and hope
It was for a good reason
These people had turned my bleached and
Inebriated life from a game of checkers
On a loop to an ever expanding

Array of dimensions through
Which we do play games,
Mostly Chess and Go! But
The matches we participate in have apocalyptic and meteoric
Consequences too that may in time yield the most
Stunning of prizes if our collective consciousness could
Grapple furiously enough with it,
The mighty elasticity of time of which all of these bouts of
Will consist. And I'll let you know the whole time, with my heart:
The images of our love depart into the sun and that
I sit in the back seat of life, snapping pictures of you watching the road.
Keeping me safe from my own motley roadrunner imagination
Mom and dad.

A Fat Little Joke

An extra politically correct person
Can have the best of intentions
Yet still be just as hazardous as
One of those intolerant people
Constantly cracking dick jokes to the
Pretty office receptionist.
Here is how:

Think of it this way. Think World War II.
Think of the pacific theater.
Think of Imperial Japan
Here for a second.

For metaphorical purposes
Think of Harry S. Truman as the polite politically
Correct one
And the Japanese people as the bigots,
As the jokers
In history and in theory, because textbooks
Can be blurry like thick
Mycelium shaped clouds.

Sometimes an entire nation of loyal,
God fearing, hard-working, intrusively polite
Citizens, makes a joke to their king
About how each and every one of them
Is willing to hop from island to island
And die in exchange for salvation.

And the soft spoken, courteous commander
Across the ocean in America?
He makes a decision
And takes that little zinger
Far too seriously and
Hits the punch-line button first.
Boom.

Fear for all time. Cut to the laughter.

Something to Utter for Fun

It was quiet and the universe snapped its fingers
As now it was so clear, the point of what
My friends had been telling me.
It was this:
What is the best way to win
In everything, in all the world's games?
It's just to
Think clearly, but not too much.
And become he who has all-ready,
Been called the winner,
Who knows himself, and knows his fate as
The one.
You.

Eyes Closed, then Open

You are supposed to spend
The years between ages twenty and thirty
This way:
These ten years will be endured either
With the beginning of your entrance
Into the clutches of death or
With the slow, flammable realization that
You may never have to die at all.
That is if you have left enough of these little
Jokes lying about come your time to depart.
If you are succinct like death with
Your choice of words,
If you consider the macroscopic timeline
Into which you bound, live in and are snuffed
Out of, that the mixing bowl of existence around you
Is as the human world to an ant and that
Our time may not be linear as if above and below
Our small lives, that within your very
Circulatory system, inside your fingertips,
There may be vestiges of a higher existence.
In this time in which children lose their
Youth and give away their control over the
World, you may maintain your childish ways.
And this is your maxim to the jesters and finite things
And the men of cloth telling you all of
This life is just preparation for judgement.
This is not the beginning or the prerequisite.

This moment of clarity and departure,
This is the median where you have learned to
Open

        Your

                Eyes

And wake laughing
To the Sunday hymns,
Knowing every day can be this mystic if
You just listen to the rapture well and scribble enough
To record the thing like Troy falling.

November Breaths

Mid-November air
Gnaws on the end of my chin
As I think : $9.00.
It's my budget for the week.
It's society's alms for
My prayers.
$9.00.
$9.00. That's enough
To be the kind of person
Who knows a two-quarter-cup
Of coffee, a bowl of chopped
Expired, frayed, stale lettuce
And rancid Kroger turkey
From a ziplock bag
Will let him live and be the kind
Of man I'd like to be.
Now, in the short term, handfuls
Of pocket change, caffeine
And grinning rage will
Wake me up
Each day.
With
The
Sun.

Your Last Words

"Can I have some
Fry bread, Matthew?",
My sick, starving
Half-dead granny
Asked with a whimper.
Her eyes sunk deep in
Her face.
Her brown skin taut
Over her high cheekbones
Like canvas on a drum.
The cancer in her corneas.
The blooming contusion on
Her brow from bouncing
Her head off of the kitchen floor.
Weak knees, balance lost
Forever.
And my mom's mom made
Me remember:
You aren't from those Black Hills, boy.
You are a part of them as
You will be even after
They're gone again.

And I too know that kind
Of "watching you die" feeling.
It is in my guts before breakfast
Every day. I take it out on wage

Work and hard plucked pentatonic
Blues scales till the nickel wound
E string of the flimsy guitar snaps
And that destructive
Force makes your song even
More beautiful.

Knowing the Difference

On a whim as a social experiment
Today, a man strolled into
His minimum wage job wearing
A suit and tie with wingtip
Polished dress shoes while everyone
Else wore their smocks, non-slip
Clod-hoppers and suicidal frowns
On their sullen faces.
The man meanwhile, just smiled
And knew that the single solitary
Difference between him and the
Boss was about four dollars,
Fifty cents and a sense of
Authority. Which the man now
Had too. All for the fun of it.
Just for a laugh.

Reality Shrugs Its Shoulders

The moment my right ring finger
Started looking like my crazy uncle James
Was when the apophenia* began to take hold.
Could be I had a keen eye for
Recognizing recessive traits passed onto me.
Could be the hunk of fatty skin that rolled
Over my fingernail, underneath my cuticle
Really did look like a drunkard who burned
His house down with his wife inside. And
I was seeing my own future going up in flames.
Could be this was my way of spotting my
Own impending loss of grip on what
Psycho-analysts try to call reality.
Or in that small instant it became apparent,
In all my quests to find meaning in every fiber of
Everything in existence, I saw it:
In all we see, we search for patterns. Even if they
    aren't there.
Some of us find them anyway, though they are
    invisible to all others.
Some of us never can reach Heaven like that.
Others, looney tunes like us, keep looking.
Regardless of all in the background
Shrugging their shoulders and shaking pill bottles
In our general direction.
Our half smile at the ready
Being content with the twirling logarithms and neon Cyrillic
Dancing in front of our eyes.

Apophenia is a psychological phenomenon whereupon the individual inflicted perceives patterns and connections withing a great deal of their every day life. These patterns often give the person delusions and exacerbate maniacal behavior in those who experience bi-polar depression. Apophenia is a known symptom of the early onset of paranoid schizophrenia.

Sense For No One But You

As the thought of you faded
And the dreams of us stopped
And I forgot what your face looked like
And your voice left me forever,
I remembered to stop and cast away all else
To simply
Make something good right now, to write a song, to splatter India
Ink on Washi paper in a language not my own,
And try to crack the Earth with my dyslexic way of speaking in riddles
For we are all at the feet
Of purple mountains lost, deaf, and incapable of speaking because
The tunnel vision of the epiphany of you was too much
For our eyes.
This is the point of entry.
The deviation of scrawled red and blue
Pastel crayon on allegoric walls with words that don't make
Sense in any language but yours.
I lost you and fumbled everything else
Trying to catch a glimpse of you
Again. And time stopped because
You were so far away. Oceans far gone
Maybe somewhere past Neptune I think
Perhaps my ways of carpet-bombing and hurricanes on a whim

Hurled you to interstellar space, away from my kind and all
 we know
But still,
Your gift to me:
The words
That never stopped
Coming.

Your Reincarnation in a Tanka

You came back something.
Was it the railroad tracks I'm
Walking? The brittle
Leaves? Or the ink of these words?
Either way, I feel you here
Writing, living on for them.

Something Novel

You knew what my name
Meant. Though I had never
Met you. You read the same books
As I did.
You knew that wisdom was
A Secret only to be passed
On. That though your life's
Love fades
And history erases you.
The steadfast man survives
It. And what of
The bird shitting on his arm?
It's all a triviality.
To him.
To us all.
To me.
Nothing simply cannot
Be wiped away.
Perhaps even
The sun
By something
In the name
Of enough gods.
Or by me with an incantation
Of something inspired by
The fleeing
Memory of
You.

Words For a Boy

Even though the son
Is born after, and of
Her.
Even though generally our
Progeny require a
Spark, a night
Of hard love,
A commitment, a
Ring, a
Lie or two, a
Signature and dick-headed
In laws, a baptism with
Child-support thrown in
Even though nothing
Is for sure:
There are others who
Came to be of their own
Volition.
Spontaneously combusting
Out of the Republic as it
Turned back to slavery.
And though they were absent
Minded their own enslavement
He battled on from that.
From retardation
From surviving the drugs
From the world declaring no

And him contemplating yes.
From a collective societal orgasm
And his eternal celibacy.
From their cultural fibromyalgia
And his quasar-giant smile.
From being fired from one job
And creating infernos in the other.
This is independence. Knowing
Your small revolutions that crept up
Just now under the Main street bridge

With the hobos and their never
Ending joints and those were your
True friends. Their existence defined
Your transiency. That you weren't illiterate
The way they the prophets said.
This time in purgatory, it would free you
Knowing god had cast out such heartless
Ideas and isolation killed other men.
But not you, my sun. And that word, son, harkens
Back to where we all began and you were
The sun. The sun.
That bright obelisk in my sky.
The sun.
The sun.
My son.
It would free you.
All these books and words and kennings
That came from I don't know where.
And ignition would come
As we prayed.

Fixing Things Means Freedom

One man breaks the button
Off his jeans and tosses
Them into the garbage.
Others sew it back on again
Or better yet, hoist their grimy
Jeans up with a bit of twine
In the belt loops. Or using a zip
Tie or rubber band, forgets they
Were ever broken at all. Going
About their day.
Liberated.
Having become something more
Than average or the mathematical mean
From the rest of men.
The independent one knows
What his heart needs, to
Stop throwing all of life's garments away,
To keep knowing it is he of an iron will
That embraces the forever flowing nature
Of all, including the split,
The deviation in time where one of us gives up
And the other treads on, his ripped pants
Rustling toward the sun set.

A Signal

She has one hand on the steering
Wheel. The other wraps a cigarette
In her fist. Eighty miles
An hour in tearing rain.
Eyes on a cell phone in her
Lap. Eyes enveloped by wires
And speakers billowing gray
Meaningless voices from
Some other end of the Earth.
Her thoughts on all other times
But this one. On tomorrow she
Contemplates, never aware.
Breaths rasping, bones calcifying too much
And frail, her attention everywhere in all
The world except for where
The road is taking us now.
Blind that vanity might act
To crash this car and tumble
Us both off into the highway 254
Ditch where we'll become little
Honorific crosses and mama,
We aren't even Christian.
We're something older that
This world forgot about centuries
Ago on purpose. And it's all somewhere
On this little electronic pocket square, filed away
The obituaries of our mothers who came before.
But for now avert your eyes more
From distraction. Look toward my

Outstretched thumbs up and move
Forth. Toward not my fingers
But where the moon really sits waiting for us
Where we stand to live forever,
Singing folk songs and dancing
With whiskeys to the end. To that fate
Of the endless dance let's ride with
Your focus on the song and eyes forward as we
Replace Crazy Horse and Sitting Bull with Twitter feeds.

Existence of Robinson Jeffers

Think back to when we built houses using
Beached stones we'd dragged off after
Swims in the sea which is so near
Us. There was no running water,
No lights to speak of.
No plugins, no wires at all.
Just a range for cooking and
A table, and perhaps a cot in
The corner to sleep in from
Time to time.
It was then under these humble
Circumstances that we were truly
Free from the world which was all
About telling us we needed to
Grow up and learn the technological
Prowess of it all and there I was
Whittling my pencil back sharp
Again. Knowing that to go off of time's
Radar was my overlying goal in life.
Amidst the naturally analog. The hardwood
Natural finish of my existence.

Laughing Over Sake

A priest in Kansai Japan
Winked at me and passed a highball
Whiskey with a smile.
I took the whole cup. One swig.
He knew I was in trouble
Yet handed me another,
Laughing because there's nothing
Else one can do save for tip
Glasses to your suffering.
Sharing a moment while the sun runs
Away until spring and waiting till it
Comes back
Around with the warmth again.
Drunk and cold, emanating heat
With a shit eating grin
Knowing Satori
We prayed.

God Help the World

Do you
See the bruise on my gut?
The one below my ribcage?
That looks like liquid mercury
And spilled melted lead?
It's brown-grey-blue and horrifying.
You know the one.
I hope you do.
Did you know it started growing
When all the people I loved kicked
Me in the chest while I was writhing on
A dirt floor crying like an infant?
Did you know I liked it when they
Eviscerated my body and that the small
Tears dripping from my laughing face
And the sound of steel toe boots meeting my
Torqued abdomen, the thunder of my heart
Pumping in my ears and my temples,
The joy of it?
That it was a symphony to me?
Being stamped out was the second
Coming of Jesus Christ to me.
So you see it. Right? Here is what
I want you to do now. Because this contusion
That never goes away, it was bludgeoned
Into me and now I'm in love with that action,
And it does hurt like god.

But make a fist now.
One like a stone and jab it with all
You have, right there
In the bruise I love so much,
In the hole where my spleen used to be.
Rape my skin with your hands and make me
Stronger.
Get me good and wild because
I don't think you can handle it
And if you can…
God help the world.

The Minor League

I'd rather whiff at
A Randy Johnson slider in Heaven
Then never have the nerve
To walk through the stadium gates
And onto the field in the first place.
It reminds me of the hanging curve ball
My grandfather threw me during batting
Practice one afternoon when I was thirteen
After I had been cut
From the freshman baseball team and how
My bat whammed it over the left field fence.
All he did was raise his eye brows,
Saying nothing.
Though I knew it was a homer.
The point?
Swing hard. It will make your arms
Stronger for chopping wood
Later on in some form
Of the afterlife.

A Further Maxim

I do feel you now as the rain
Falls and Winter sets in to test
Me in all of this. In which hemisphere,
Which country, what time-zone
You are staying in at the moment,
I have no glint and no right to know
Anymore.
Though I am smoldering convinced
Forever you appeared to me in order
To confirm through grace alone all our
Small battles can be won. That faith
Was something to harness and aim directly
Inward towards one's heart. That dreams
Are and were as real as we needed them
To be, given the rubber banding nature
Of our alliterative jokes. Punishment barraging
From without, but unbelievably so from
Within for if we could take the blame
For all the world's wars, we most certainly
Would.
In these, my great friend, my love,
You were my teacher and wherever,
Whenever you are, these maxims are woven
For you.

Waka on Hui Neng

Beware the free lunch,
Hui Neng* used to say. I thought
That's true. Unless you
Speak the bartender's language.
Then it's free on principle
Because you struck his
Heart lightly with your fist.

Hui Neng is the sixth patriarch of the Chinese Chan sect of Buddhism. He was a major proponent of the sudden enlightenment method of attaining access to the realm of Nirvana.

Day 1: My Friend The Dying Mouse

Today from the dirt below the foundation of my rolling trailer home, you, a field mouse, found the crack, the small yet just large enough hole to crawl your way through to my non-insulated, non-draining, non-used, caulk-less, paintless death beige, plastic bathtub.

The little hole in my shower, in my dirt and mung encrusted wash bin is where you saw the light for winter. It's where you were born again, resurrected out of the cold only to become trapped in my washroom with no way in the world to get out. That is unless I scooped your keychain size body up in a Pepsi can and threw your cute ass in the garbage.

So this was your first day in my world, little trapped mouse. With your little black eyes and your bitsy curvy tail. You were my prisoner and I would enjoy keeping you a while. To be my confidant. My friend. Four walls, the crack you squeezed through for salvation and that you'd never find your way out of again. These were my musings. The drain with its teeny pie shaped screen holes you'd try and seize your body through in order to flee into the sewage tomorrow for a new second coming too.

And me, I was your scribe, the master of your chain of events and the future's knowledge of you. It made my heart jovial to be your personal rodent biographer.

Day 2: Your Death, Resurrection, and the Key Lime

You were Kareem Abdul-Jabbaring your way up the sides of the tub last night, but I think you knew. There was no escaping this now. Babies, as you, can't wail so sonically loud in ache for return to the womb that they can travel back. They are like you my friend whose tail out-lengths your body. You'd never be outside again where you belong. As the baby can never travel back to its mother's chalice, you were doomed to living in my domicile's pooper.

I left you scrambling for freedom with no food and no friends, just darkness and your fading sense of hope. As if mice have that kind of human distinction to hold on to in the face of death. You probably just accepted that dreadful decision to ascend into my world, your hell. Either way, this was your Thermopylae. And as the Spartans, when I came back in the morning to piece it all together, you had lost. This must be how it felt to be Persian, I thought. Looking at all that Greek death. You were slaughtered as them, splayed out for me to see the history of your fight. And I would worship you.

I saw your mouse sized scratch marks on the shower drain. So in the night you fought it, your small war against starvation. The one you so cleverly made for yourself by barging into my home.

To confirm your appearance of having lost all in the night, I kicked the toe of my moccasin loafer into the plastic on the side of the water basin once. Nothing. You really were gone, I thought. Deceased. Dead mouse toast. But I had to be sure. I kicked the tub again and as soon as my foot met the hollow sounding place where you kicked rocks to the afterlife the night before...Your tail unfurled and twitched wildly into a bee line as your brown cotton ball body writhed ferally. Your body looked like a baby's arm grabbing hold of a live spark plug.

A miniscule squeak alarmed from your little mouth.

Half a second of life. And you died again back into your plush rodent coma. You were a miniature beady eyed vegetable. A baby potato of a thing. Half way to house-pest heaven. I could see you were still fighting.

Before bed, I'd been eating a Key lime slice I'd snagged from atop a fruit cake. It was Christmas time and we were jolly outside the bathroom door. We celebrated while you were encapsulated, swinging between this life and the next in your mouse-sized intensive care unit where I wash my balls and armpits. Where I meditate in the bathwater and am only interrupted by my own curious flatulence. Rip. This is where your deathbed would be.

     With a slice of Key lime. A morsel of hairy fruit for a lifetime. I threw it in the tub next to your limp body the way a passerby tosses a dime into a homeless fellow's guitar case. Best of luck. You are wretched. You are doomed. You are lifeless, septic, cancerous and blind. Yet your music is beautiful if you are the guitar man. But with you, my friend. There was no music. No beauty. Just the yellow hissing song of the tank behind the toilet after I flush it and exit.

Day 3: Your Life Returned and I Misunderstood

And so there I left you, assuming my offering of sustenance was just a tribute to you. As if I had left flowers for a soon to be flatliner. Then you were alone in the dark again with drips of trickling, filthy sink water instead of electronic beeps coming to a crawl, confirming your trip to mouse hell. Because let's be real, you did break into my house and in my religion, mice who enter without permission are sent directly to House-Pest Hades upon cessation from this world.

And you slept.

Then the sun rolled back around. Morning came and it was time for my dawn time dump.

I sauntered into the bathroom and you were gone. Vanished. I was beside myself and couldn't help but think about how all of man kind's religions might explain how you, an infinitesimally squeaky rodent of a thing could cheat death this way.

Buddhists, from wherever they come, tell me that life comes down from heaven in cycles. That time drips upon us and can stretch about the landscape, convincing us all of this life must be relatively linear.

Catholics, in my neck of the woods, tell me a virgin can give us god from her womb and that all of this is a miracle from outside the bounds of man's rules and laws.

Atheists, with their cynicism and bloat, inform me that none of this means anything at all.

And they all applied to you, this animal that refused to move on to the next life.

And somehow, none of them can provide me with the answer as to how you, my black-eyed mouse buddy, found his way out and survived this three-day ordeal, which was supposed to kill you. Was it that the Key lime was some kind of miracle cure for mice and granted you super-rodent abilities to escape man's wash bins? Is it as if citrus fruit is a form of Sensu-savior for you animals?

I don't know anymore and that seems okay to me.

What are the consequences of not understanding anyway? Is there a fatal symptom to not knowing? Can my friend, the house pest, be revered for having eluded my sense of superior human logic and David Blained his way home back outside? Again, I don't know.

Perhaps my roommate used the bathroom that last night, was horrified and twirled you right down the toilet with a shriek as your eulogy.
Never will I know.
And that
Is
Fine.
Just know, I could worship you. A Rodent like Jesus. A crumb nibbling

       Floor dweller just like Mohammed.

Ways to Find Her Again

She died alone and I know yet again,
Just about everything you did,
My friend. Not all.
But enough. That this one
Needed to be written down
First and neatly. It was merely the
Next moment that was exactly the
Point. What needed to be damned
To all of it, Except you:
Was irrelevant. But we all
And I mean all of us
Lost Her too, my friend.
And so you were never
Alone.
I, in
Ink pen curvy
Bold
Letters
Say
From
The
Other
Side:

We all witnessed
It.
And she said, "I love you too".
In her own fucked up way.
From next to the sun up there in…Heaven?

But then
I don't and can't really know though
Just for now. But maybe after a while
We will see it, her face in the clouds and her voice
Carrying in the
Wind on our way
Up.

And the Weather

Without us
It began to feel as though the flint rocks beneath my feet
Were speaking of death, telling me that hell was rising and the
   tumbling
Stones were clashing together at all times throughout the day
   and in
The beginning every inebriated human intersection
Was preceded in this boy's head by
The opening riff of a George Thorogood
Song - Like drinking alone
It was all of it at the very end we decided
Just how all of this would end up:
An impromptu made up spur of the moment
Cobalt bombing with
Kerouac Jazz as the soundtrack as I smoked
Joints without filters and endured
Hangovers cured with warm orange juice and beer.
That was the idea. For this ditty is about the recovery period
   from you,
Where the lyricist spends nights in jail and accepts
Salvation to be that note in the song he can't help but
Scratch the diamond needle back to on the phonograph because
   it reminds him of it all.
And this was the poet growing into a man, sick knowing
That the color black is hardly the darkest of shades

One can imagine. Hearing comets of plutonium-239 and razor blade tumble to Earth
And watching as hurricanes made of sulfur and rape make land fall
In his mind through the weeps of twelve string guitars.
The nicotine smell of the end of the world made this day after
A night of drinking feel like crucifixion and an orgasm with
Botticelli. So the sound of stones crashing, The Sistine Chapel crumbling,
And the smell of The Birth of Venus on fire,
The curators watching and wailing as the history of this art dies onward
Is what recovery felt like to the bard whose eyes saw nothing but
Flames and smelt only fumes that made his body shake
Amid the prayer,
This song. No rhyme and no tempo. No pulse. Yet somehow alive. Bathed in sweat
Praying to nothing in particular, just pursuing the source
Of this work again, the combination of paint and foreplay
That made my body ache high the way it did then because of
 the burning Mona Lisa of
You.

Just the Next One

A guy I work with in the textile warehouse
A kid really I find him to harbor artistic intelligence,
I should add. It was a worldliness I didn't
Know at that age.
In the office where mainly clothing, and sweaty
T-shirts are priced and shipped back to Lima
Or Bangladesh or where ever in the world they
Came from. To Mexico City or Osaka?
I haven't a clue anymore and
Wouldn't care if it mattered. These bits of
Clothing I've seen, whether my friend wore
Them or all my enemies, it felt exactly the same.
We all seemed to be barking at something.
All the time.
Together.

Where cheaply made, outsourced articles were
Our trade, one day, we found
A ragged, duck-taped together
Cardboard box.
An awkward, big-heavy son of a bitch
Situation with haggard post office stickers
Attached from everywhere on it. It was all for us.
The long-haired slacks wearing boy, my
New friend, opened the smelly box and
And suddenly he wasn't at work anymore.
It was a mix of big honking thick, beautiful

Books: A Charles Frazier first edition
Stolen from a library, a leather bound
collection of Emerson essays and editions of Baldwin
Poetry. It seemed as something of a warehouse
Miracle, the chance of it, that someone would
Dump a truckload of knowledge in such a way.
My friend took the especially throat cutting books
Home with him that day. Insubordinate theft be damned.
I thought I'd never see him again.
He came back the next day beaming.

Happy New Year Calendar Prayer

These squares we pray to.
Arabic numerals blocked
In those black lines that tell us
The roaring twenties are back
Again. They have me contemplative
And I wonder why we rely on these
Pieces of paper and black ink to tell us where
We are and how much time we
Have left.

A couple books, untold gallons
Of wine, daily maniacal rage bouts,
And after having one wife disappear
At the frenetic nature of my existence
Here I am indeed,
Still worshiping the rule
The page, the sun and myself.
And the moon too and I know
These have power yet to be drawn.

The cycle of it. It's the pen shaking
As I write this that I find truly frightening
And affirming that all of this life is real.
That we should fear the next word,
The next question, next action,
Next moment, next year, is what should
Tell you, the green light for life
Is always on and never truly changes to red
The way man's laws tell us it should.

All of your love molotov cocktailed
And gone? Trip to the police pokey
Looming and your bank account
Stymied at $0.93? Salty sweat rolling
On your palms?
Start loving it.
Happy new year,
Pain.
We're still here.

No Consideration Necessary

Your journal should not be considerate of others.
This is the selfish act you can justify without
Question. No need for tact now. If you've cheated
Here, bludgeoned something to death there, these
Blue ruled lines are the places to proclaim it, be
Proud of it. Be willfully prideful of your fury.
Do you think a typhoon or a twister hesitates?
You shouldn't either. Never burned will you
Become inside your own rambling thoughts. Because
Let's be honest with this thing. Depravity right now
Is often lauded after a few centuries or so I think.
Or turned to doctrine after the creator martyrs
Themselves.
So here. Right here. In ink.
Say it. Spill it like the world depends
On you meaning it.
Be zealous in your Morning-Star-like
Barbarisms. And you do exhibit many of them. This
Small note to yourself is where ego is allowed to
Ignite. So now, let it out before you annihilate
Or obliterate something that can throw you away
Behind bars or put you in a padded room forever.

A Text Message For Kate

You may not have noticed the whole thing
At all. But in case you did, to clear up any ideas
You had about how I may be stalking you,

I promise you, Kate.

It was really just a wild coincidence
That I came walking out of the bicycle
Shop when you were heading into the
Hookah bar next door where we used to sit and
Read together, way back, before our
Miniature interpersonal no survivor car crash took
Place. Our mini-Holocaust made for two.
It was nothing. I needed a new chain. A new sprocket
For my bike. That is it.
Today we won a lottery together. No payout.
Only pain. For me that is.

I agonized over even sending this text.
So in the end, I resolved not to. To leave
You alone, and delete the pixelated
Evidence after I'd written it down in
My notebook. For a poem of course, But
More so as to remind myself I
May have done the right thing for a
Change, and let it be. Let you be. Let us be.

Though in that sand grain moment it
Was easy to consider staging my
Own little Blitzkrieg to embarrass you in public as
If I hadn't in front of the whole world already.
Because you looked back at
The little blue car I was sitting
Behind the wheel of as you
Made for the bar's front door.
Looking at me perhaps not knowing it.
My heart had turned into a Black Flag song
As you walked. And Before I pulled away, your eyes met
Mine, through the black tinted windows.
Like you did know…Like the cosmos knew.

I wanted to roll down the driver's side window and shout:
"Hey, Mama, K! Long time, No?!"
And pop the clutch hard and
Fish tail it out of there, letting you
Know I'd been there
Barbaric and loud,
Like before.
But I didn't.
Couldn't. Knew it would scar
The already sulfur thick
Air between us.

I knew what might have been there when
We were younger, what we called unconditional
Love, dumber and unwittingly naive then, it was gone.
Or at least lost somewhere

On the big celestial playground we have been chasing each other
On. Like hand-written letters we were a lost art.
But still,
The cycle of it
Worldly things, I mean and their propensity for
Harkening back to their unadulterated
Points of origin, back home.
It magnetized our eyes for
Some psycho-algorithmic oddball reason
As if you were north
And I south,
We would go into eternity
Smacking into one another from
Time to time.
Despite the downed larch trees on
All life's roads. We kept on scaling them.
In counter to all logic
Through the bloody mycelia,
through the smashed dinner tables at Thanksgiving
And over the hills and far away I guess.
I saw you then. And now
Until this.
All ends again.
Life, I mean. You're just there, not physically.
Just like the stars that aren't really there anymore.
Like light that went out a millennia ago.
Like you, I mean.

The Game Unto Work

Being poor, the game
Most of us seem to lose at
Or die in prisons
At the end of or stop dreaming because of
Within it? Dreams shade my eyes
And this winter, I change the definitive or the dreams to
Reality. I open my middle eye.
I also change the meaning of frigid to mean
It is no longer cold on my skin.
To fair weather I migrate.
Smiling, sleeved in
The morning flurries
Striding into the office
At ease.
Poor because society demanded it.
Rich because the nature of things willed it.
I am happy because my body felt it,
That I wasn't in fact
Dead from
Clocking
In.

A Photo of Me Psychoanalyzed

(A Black and White Self-Portrait)

A monochromatic print of me
Snarling with giant headphones covering
Wild unkempt hair. My dimple the
Only bit of innocence in the
Image.

I think
This is me expressing
Myself.
This is happy.
This is my black and white
Robert Adams lunatic
Sonnet writing face.
This is me letting you hear it
That I know about the middle way
Between one hell and another.
That I am not an elephant knocking
At your big
Red door,
That I, despite my Neapolitan oak
Bookcase made by me,
And all its tomes of classic liberalism,
I am no blue jackass either.
You should know that.
It is so important for approaching me,
To know that I am not something

You will find a definition
For in no dictionary
And nothing in your King James
Bible or your big leather-bound DSM-5
Is going to cure me. Because
What I have is truly black
To You.
The enemy you must incarcerate,
The one you'd incinerate if you could,
Me.
I am your unknown variable
The remainder you can never justify
Or solve for.
Oh and entropy?
That endless doomsday warhead
That big Caesar Bomba?
That is me!

So please, please know all of this.
It is in your interest
And that if you have to ask me
What it is that I am
Then you have already lost
This round of the game.

But it is okay.
Because the game,
This pastime
Most of us make pennies and gulp
Pabst Blue Ribbons for

It unfolds on a loop
For all time, princess.

So, Better luck next time.

Hopefully you haven't been brought back
As a Durian fruit
By the next time we meet.

You might be one of the those raunchy,
Hairy, kudamono of Indo-China
One day in the next
Kalpa life.

If that's the case, If I have to
Spend an entire lifetime stinking
To high hell, I have to say,
That is mighty fine by me!

How about you?
Again my friend, This? This feral
Grey matter? This is happy.
My true enraged enamourment.

A Kind of Popular Thought

People think you have to jot about psychosis
In dimly lit Cafes as you sip brands of
Espresso I can't pronounce in order to make art.
But a man or a woman in poverty using
Some kind of of fucked up writing
Utensil, preferably something stolen or
Picked up out of the gutter or the mud, can snap their
    grimy fingers
And with their super-power, vagrant transiency,
Can wiggle their wrist and flick the
Lights of the world right on.
With
        Emphasis needed, friends.
No $8.45 venti soy mocha necessary.
And when your eyes are open and you are
Beside yourself with hunger, a lout for food and
Enlightenment, the whole planet with its poets and
    cartographers
With no work left to do. It becomes the cup from
Which you can drink forever and still have
Quite nothing at all save for
This quietude of life.
And that is the reward
For this art
You make.

A Sense of the Wild

Oh my god! They all said at the
Boy's inherent and degenerate sense
Of wilderness, that to him there
Was no outdoors or outside
That there seemed in his mind
To be no split there. We
Were just all varying gauges
Of steel, nickel wound guitar strings
Vibrating at different pitches.
And again. Oh my god! They diagnosed
As if the concept of a Catholic fellow
Re-corking the infinite number of revelations
Streaming from the wine bottle of truth
We all tirelessly gawk at with wide eyes,
As if this simple man's dream were impossible
And they missed what the point was
Messing about with their doctrines.

A Nostalgic Treatment

Needing
To go back
And have an IV drip
Of all the music
You listened to as
A seething, randy, thirteen
Year old junior high kid.
That may help you revert for
A time right now.
Such a thing may be the vitamin
You desperately
Need that just may enable
You to get back in touch with
The parts about
Yourself, like ghosts behind eyes,
That you hated back then.
Yet, distillations of which now
May save your very life
And bring about
Your next little crusade.
Who knows? The main point being
It's not the forever loss of me you are crying over
Tonight. I think it's just
That in these moments those
Corny songs we all loved
May prove vital to you,
To all of us.

A Working Lesson

The greatest thing being a laborer
Ever taught me was this:
Small things, intangible footnotes, grains of
Nothing in particular. That time you stole a Big Mac
While on the clock when it was going to get
Thrown in the garbage any way, or you didn't,
Things so infinitesimal most of us never bat an eye?
As if one hamburger nicked, that was
Raised on a field in Australia would ever cost a suit anything
At all.
They don't matter really.
But with them, some of us have learned
To somehow start to rule the whole world
From under desk lamps, atop
Natural ebony wood writing desks, books wide
Open after our nine-hour shifts, quills
A sweeping at the page. Because enough
Yellow-red visor wearing
Shift manager slash slave drivers
Have taught us without ever knowing it.
The chattel weren't enslaved anymore
Once you gave them a
Grammar book or a newspaper
Or he stole a copy of
Pilgrim's Progress from the book store.
Because some small crimes,
Weren't they just worth the cost of admittance?

Once the field worker, the cotton picker
The chicken fry fryer
The McNugget dipper
The sandwich artist
Started reading the fine print on his own
The boss was in big trouble.

A Librarian's Advice

Here is what she, the absolutely
Well read, economical, intentional, patient
Librarian told me regarding my poem reading habit
Like a slow burning star, one like maybe ours inside
Mercury's orbit sitting there, a truth for me to
Consider heeding. She told me with penetrating, concerned eyes
And pleaded with me as I rocked sweating over
A Simic collection behind the library circulation desk:
"It is one poem a day that will keep the white
Coats away. To read just one daily for some, that may be
Just okay."
For the consumer reader, his mouth full of hay
I thought maybe this could be so.
But me? I take a vitamin each dawning day
In tercet form because in focused rage, with these
Poems constantly underneath my arms, I have
A few new, cutting things to say.

A Man Like an Arrow

A good functioning, high-caliber human being,
In my under-educated opinion, should probably be
Behaving and operating Just like a well fired
Arrow from a longbow.
At all times he is working, if that is, he is working well.
Why? You might inquire.
Well, you see it's all about energy, your
Energy and where it comes from, where it goes and
What it ultimately becomes. And how it's always
Switched to the on position.
How does that pointed stick of timber
Flying for elk heart penetration act with such
A volitional action like a well polished
Symphonic movement?

First, the ranger became hungry,
And was running low on protein with which to fuel
    himself and his family.
So he left his village before dawn
Hours before sunlight woke up.
He fled, his blood sugar at war with his spirit, but his
    heart still
Ambulating for sustenance and he did find it.
In a clearing.
Like himself, just waiting for the sun, a four legged
Something or other that would feed his family
For months.

And from his feet, from the ground, all the way from the core
Of the Earth, he transferred a force of kinetic power
Through his shoulders, through his biceps, funneled
That ignition to his fingers, pulled the
Bow string back, intermediating something like god
From the entirety of the land right into the arrow,
To the bow and the string's sinew.
And maybe the unknowing ranger was a sort of mystic,
An alchemist of creating something from nothing in these woods.
And for him the meat was the gold in the transaction.
And in that instant he materialized that energy out of
Seemingly nothing.
And the people ate, and dined on the example the arrow sets.
Move forth, overcome, yielding to nothing.
And more, if an arrow flying through the air hits a
Raindrop on its way to annihilation of its target, or crosses the path
Of a stray mosquito,
It just keeps on riding the air.
The same can be said for a human being who is unmoving, unwavering
In the face of great obstacles and adversity.

And so, like the arrow, you get all of your power,
And that is most definitely what you have,
From somewhere,
Somewhere that is balanced and surely benevolent that you tap into
Each day without truly realizing it unless your heart
Is quiet, your voice is silent and your spirit is willing
To listen for it.

A Bit of Time By God

If god drew up plans
For this wound up planet with its storms
And pandemic diseases
Ho most certainly needed grunts
To carry out his typhoons and sicknesses.
He would have needed men and women
He knew would raze
And rebuild, cleanse, then repeat it all
In the name of the lord god himself.
The knowing son of a bitch.
He would have needed some kind of grunt.
Some enlistee, someone bruised and cut up
But a being moving forth like lightning
On a Thompson gun round.
Someone dangerously cat-like in his actions
Someone with one too many questions at all times
After bearing witness to all of god's plagues,
Even though such a thing lands some outside
The gates of all salvation.
Someone he needed and he unfairly received.
Some boy.
Some grunt.
Like you, my friend.

Your Thoughts on me Staring

"Define periphery for me will you, boy that is spotting
Me from the corner of your curious
Turned on eye?

What is it you keep around you, in
Your wild uncontrolled orbit that makes all the
STEM deans and logicians mash
Their neurons together and come up
With the elegant yet simple solution
To just call you a Nutrageous bar?

How are you an anomaly to them?
In a black tie yet covered in red flannel
I spot it as your wrist wriggles against
The pleads of your work trousers. It is
A top of a paper in a journal in your lap
Slightly above the belt line of the pants you've
Been peacocking around in all day. It
Was the secret, a little slip of note stationary
With a number written on it you were
Afraid to show all of us. Like you were
Linus and your little sheets of note paper
Are your safety blanket. It was the game
You've been playing with yourself and all
Others, the one where you pretend to
Be socially acceptable, despite yourself.

I say these things to myself knowing you are
Just a man, just a poet of god, that nothing more
Will happen. It is just seeming quite the good
Idea to peck you on the forehead just now
Because of all your fear and burden.

Then for some reason I imagined everything
Around you burning down in one big ball
Of flame and resolved to never be a part of
It in even any small way."

I thought of you saying these things to me
And it aroused me to know my coworkers
Were so witty inside their own heads and
Thought enough of me to think I was capable
Of that kind of overwhelming fire.

The Treaty Table

And now I heard them
A thousand fires burning
In your heart leading you
Away from me. They were the
Same flames that led me east
With the sun. And I understand
That one flick of the penned wrist
Could take you, miss. That one
Note of my deviation could
Imbed my being an orphan for
A lifetime.

Our people too
Fueled that fire and
Are dying for tonight
But not if we show up to fight.
Through this, our deepest
Great depression,
If we bring here
To the bargaining table, all our will,
Foregoing all treaties,
Putting our souls at stake
To survive.

Then I could love you a
Lifetime if you were willing
To accept my waging of war,
My fight. That my people were
Good, you could enshrine.

Birth in Terms of a CPU

Well, here's how I see a new baby in 2020.
Every time one is born, updated software
Is being surgically unpackaged by
A fellow with no hard hat on, just calipers.
So he or she better be handling the
Unit carefully because if you bounce
That new and bright, expensive toy
Off of the floor a time or two
Or a hundred because of your maternal
Depression and buyer's remorse later on
In that kid's life it will probably
Experience a few good size glitches and/or
Unexpected crashes that might land him
And his fried circuit board in prison or
With another set of wires attached to his
Forehead, threatening to revoke all his
Calculating abilities for the rest of time.
So....Cannot compute due to excess of
Emotionally inflicted terrorism.
Error code 082493.

Apology to All My Broken Watches From Childhood

Breaking you was the
Hardest thing I ever had
To do each summer
With the idea you might,
With all your component parts,
Telling me just how long I had
Before granny would bitch slap
Me for being late to dinner, how you might
End up far beyond simply shattered
Because of me.
And as a millennial
Boy frustrated by the hard
Constraints of a pocket watch or
A rubber Timex I bounce around
The floor in silent rampage
Always attempting to destroy
And disassemble and rebuild that
Which can never be taken apart
Because in the end you were all
Put together by the real clock makers
Who knew it. Certain cogs and pulleys
And parts simply survive it all.
And I look down to my bare left wrist in
A silent guilt, knowing that only
A fool is left without a sense of time.
I don't feel a cuff around my hand anymore

And know some things are too good
For foolish fools in constant rage.
And I apologize to the whirring of
A ceiling fan and the wind.

My Pulpit as It Is Now

You preach to me now the words, O sir
That you know come from your lord,
Which really only fell from the sky
All on their own and by some chance
Gave me and all the others
The great big cosmological knuckle
Sandwich that tastes so good
We call it life.

And to be beat up by this life was to
Know you had banged up a few of this
World's rules enough to make a difference.
To know you were some kind of tough
Guy, that was all secondary.
To know you had the ability to make other
People
Realize their own strength now, that
Was the truly miraculous end result.
You aren't god. That's ridiculous.
God is truly a concept by which we construe
All the suffering and death we are daily
Faced with. But of this be sure, my friend.
You are godly in your conduct and
That is what we strive towards.

And Grand Dad Collected Used Golf Balls

Of many colors all from
The bottom of the water hazard
On the ninth hole of the public
Golf course, Nikes, Spaldings, Pings,
The occasional Tiger model or Gold Bear,
You collected them all granddad and
Bigoted as you might have been
The day I stole your golf cart and intentionally
Crashed it into the creek at the
Age of seven, I feel you got my point.
You taught me a valuable lesson too.
Even after your dad's dad tries to beat
You to death with a three wood, accidentally
In his back swing, from a par 5 tee box, it is
Still a life applicable one. You
Were indiscriminate with your
Treasure trove of used muddy
Golf balls. And that was the lesson you had.
I just applied that to human
Beings granddad, and you became a
Wise old man in my imagination and the
Short memory codex of my eyes. So
Thank you for being and not being
Though you died for real back
In Korea and survived long enough to
Come back and bludgeon the
Knowledge into us kids.

Bibles and Messages

The Talmud, the Torah,
The King James Bible
And even
The Sutras
The Qu'ran too.
I read them all with
Many glances and now
Know the definition
Of God might well be
Full of
Fluidity.

So it taught me this.

Play on.
Even as the rain
Rapidly turns to hail
And Kansas twisters
Because you are
On stage and
This is your
Palladium.

Life.

With the Wisdom of a Dog

I thought today my
Journey to hell might
Be started. Then
My dog greeted me
At the screen door
On my way to work.
So I plod on saving
For kibbles and bits.
Half eaten beef round-
Eye, for his love. The
Loyalty of it makes the
Stars worth seeing each
Night. His sense of smell
Becomes my sense of gratitude.
My existence comes to
Mean something more and
By synonymous congruity
With that becomes the love
Of it all, his love I mean. The
Toil metronoming back and
Forth with his dumb smile
Ever present.
Remember this day
As the day you were
No longer allergic
Or intolerant to

Anything or anyone in the world
Because of the love of
An animal.
Remember.
You could have been a fighter.
You could have been a warrior.
You could have been a paid killer.
But instead you chose in silly anger
To tread the middle path
With your wind-horse mind,
Your bear-like spirit
To walk
Taking the path of
Rocky wisdom you
Trail on. Laughing
Heartily and forever
Maniacal in your almost
Too far gone kind of way.
And smile knowing. Your teachers would
Always need wisdom far more than their
Little tests. And they would
Never have this kind of canine
Adoration from a friend.
Twiddling their calculators
And slivers of chalk.

No Tracing the Lines Now

We were poor as the dirt
And had more fun than god himself.
We built houses out of dogshit and
Lived there for years on end.
With making art we saved ourselves
Too!

No tracing for us. We always
Lived to freehand despite the mistakes,
Building castles out of karma.
Redeeming fallen friends
Without the guilt of survival. Lives
We've celebrated in each line
Would surely reach the next
Generations. We never doubted.

Proudly, we held white
Flags to all pursuers,
Plead the fifth, shut up and
Tuned the guitars, re-stringed
The violins and re-tuned the pianos
Knowing any one of us could be
Nero fiddling as the city of gold
Burned. We couldn't
Have that.
We needed home.
And the next song.

Among the Other Customers

If I
Forgot to tip
You, I apologize
But that you
Would still remember
My life would
Enamor me
For the rest of time.
It was because you
Insisted on calling
Me by my real first
Name, unlike the others.
Even outside
This diner, without
Pocket change
You said my name
And it sounded just
Like egg-white
Frittata-a-la-mode.
Your voice, like that of
A Girl's I hadn't heard
Since age twelve. It
Mused me to writing
About you here now
At your bar among
The other customers
With a thing or two to

Say of you and your
Rouged lips calling
Me sweetheart,
Giving me pancakes
Instead of love.
And they tasted good,
Like a childhood
I'm forgetting.

Considering the Alternate Drugs

To say now that coffee was the
Only antidote would be to exaggerate.
The real admission is that
It is the absolute least of all
Evils I could be imbibing.
Knowing I don't even know how
To spell some of these dandy words
I say:
Many I have known had to shoot
To snort
To mainline
To pop
To smoke
To ruin their
Jackson Pollock and
Andrew Wyeth colored lives
In order to become one with god.
But me?
I managed to weasel my way out
Of those handcuffs and straight
Jackets. Because I was scared
Enough and became good at the
Arts of escape in various forms.
And you, you had to live so badly
After your real life you
Just always lingered
Behind my eyes.

Advice to My Talkative Peer

The written word is often far
More economical and wastes
Much less energy than the loud
Combustible, noise polluting
Siren of the spoken one.
That being the case,
Please quiet yourself momentarily
And start writing brief
Letters to people, just to see what
They send back.
Because they might surprise you.
You might send a care package to
A family in a country far away and
They might, being unsuspecting
Recipients, be so moved
They send you a Christmas card
Every year for the rest of your
Life, or better, write them out in your
Language, with their
Signature in Mandarin Chinese.
The pain of it is so pretty I think.
The insularity of written letters.
Isn't it revolting? Folding up your
Thoughts that way and sending them
Off into the world? It is frightening.
And you should try it.

It seems more polite and insightful
Than simply becoming annoyed and
Telling my loud friend to
Leave me alone and shut the fuck
Up.

A Note on The Fragility of Artistic Minds

It occurs to me
Creative minds
Ought to be knowing
Their inevitable
Breaking points.
For if not danger
And sad songs on
Loops await. Because
If stars really do
Go supernova and lash
Out across the universe,
Imploding with the
Strength of a million
Billion suns, then surely
There is a human
Equivalent we see walking
The streets alone with sheets
Of verse lyrics tucked underneath
His arms. Sweating and enraged
By the stolid nature of mankind.
This comparison
Hopefully will enable us to
Realize.

The production and
Organization of things,
Including thoughts of

Artistic synthesis, are subject
To Periodic self-destruction
Sometimes
And in that instant of
Our core collapse of
Sentence fragments and polyphonic
Rupture, we ought to know on a
Non-linear time scale that
All of this disturbance could
Have been avoided with a simple
Slow
Guided
Breath.

A Varying Influence

When you find yourself
Eating dinner at the
Commune with your friends
And one is a zealot and
The other is an anarchist,
Then you know it.
You have found the balance.
Your eyes de-glaze and the
Ensuing party will be quiet
And terribly awkward for
Them both gawking yet
Immensely wild.
These iconoclasts will embark
You all on the journey to differences
Of opinion you all desperately needed.
And the sexual energy of
Disagreement will bind you
All.

A Study of You in Ink

You miss were the first
One I said these words to
And they cut you and I had
No idea. You too had a relationship
With blades, katana and emotional
Guerilla terrorism. Because those
Were our alphabet soup, our fruit
Roll-ups and Crackerjack
Box prizes, that alienation. It
Was our mutual gift to ourselves
And we shared the moment
My harp started harkening their ears.
And books of by me verses started
Piling up despite myself and your
Luck would have it, you and
Your Brownie Scout eyes, your
Now platinum black dirty blonde
Hair of silk, whatever you are
These days. I'm still there, the
Luthier journeyman and you,
The Queen of this all.

A Moment after Your Slut Funeral

It was your birthday
With you dead and gone
And I closed my eyes
Then said your name to
Be greeted with laughter
From everyone you knew
And this is my way of
Saying we loved you,
My friend.
And I went to bars and parties
Where they all had fucked
You in some way. Their smiles
Said it all. You loved them
Too and I had to accept it.
Your hookerish life translated
Into laughs for us all.
Always.

In Traffic Court Imagining My Parents Were There

And to my parents,
You lived long. You shared it
All.
Water from the spicket,
My love
Raising me
And the work
It all took
And sitting catty-corner
From me in this courtroom
You know I still love you
Both.
You really looked like them.
But then I took a self-portrait of
Us all, snapped it with
My camera and here you still
Are reminding me I
Will never be alone
In this world with you
A few steps behind,
Crying so I never
Have to. Lingering so I
Am never driving through
Life solo
My filial Confucian ditty
And all my alms are in
Dedication
To you.

To Hear the Sermon

These times we dined
In many circles of hell
Built the way in which
We live with grit.
And these pages are stained
Not with blood, but with
The fingerprints of those
Who toiled and the resins,
The leftovers of their tears
And you will never see the
Histories of these men and
Iron women in the background.
You will not see for yourself,
But you find and continue
To stumble on the many points
And voices of god!
Without preaching, I tell you,
That to hear sermons you may
Not have to attend temple
Services or Mass. Nor will
You have to face toward
Mecca or give your life for
Anything your heart deeply needs.
I can try to write this
As a matter of record, the way
Good friends banter and
Grin. For I am not god and
Neither are you. But we are
Close I think.

A Monument for Her

For Alex Buckley

You built this

Bridge that survives her, my friend and

I get to cross

It each day, stumbling with my bottomless flask

And the greatest

Saddest gift

Is I was able to watch

The steel of the beams

Oxidize, for the years were shuffling on now,

The stars a blur from down here where we laughed once. We all

Cry invisible tears remembering the eight-ball lightning of you

Because you were here

Back then

And taught us about savagery and living our lives like controlled demolitions.

I saw you bleed hallucinating

And survive

The pang of its

Construction in the spot where she died

So her heart

Might live on

And then you

Began that creeping death walk into hell

Too. A casualty of the little rattling prescription bottle war.

You blamed yourself
And I had to say it.
She had to die so that you
May have lived to
Know your spirit was
Real.

And then you
Slipped on too.
No bridges named for you.
Just baby sons of friends you made laugh too hard
Over and over.

A Wrong Choice of Words

To say fuck only. To hiss it quietly instead of laughing,
It was the wrong choice of
Words for loving torture this much that
You made back then
Many
Times
Over and under all
The
Mountains we know by heart.
We, in our arts that all our parents damned,
All Know
About the fact that
It's
Just a joke
Usually.
And you
Are the
Various
Punch Lines.
For there are many.
Se be ready
Always for
The beat that takes you
And brings down the
Hammer with a laugher
About how your stoned pinball Gameboy salvia
Sense of reality

Might as well be an
Etch-a-sketch and
You push away
All the hands
That reach
For you,
The many.
You swear at them saving you.
Screaming
Fuck you. I'm a bard. Keep lashing your whip, my love.

No War Today, Just Burnt Food and Too Many Spices

Once when I was living with a friend from Japan
We sat together eating breakfast and he
Said to me in quite good English,

"Matt San, the way you eat.
It looks like you are going
To war. Where is this war you
Are fighting?"

I looked back at my friend, halting.
Half chew.

I'd left the skillet grease
On my pork sausage, burnt it.
I'd mounded up red onion, bell
Peppers and burnt them too. On
Purpose!
I'd sprinkled a cup of jalapeño peppers
Atop the sausage rounds. It was hot.
I was hot. In a rage I wasn't aware of.

Yet my friend understood clearly.
And he saw it that through both of our
Languages.
Even in seeming calm my mind
Was shipping off to battle and

It wasn't a monoglot situation.
All he had to do was look at the
Fury of my habits
On a daily basis.

He saw that I liked to suffer,
That it put a wild smile on my face to feel pain,
That it was dangerous for anyone around me
To be there for.
Yet he sat there at the breakfast table with me
An equal in the war of seclusion we both seemed to know.

Something Small

It's the small things, friend.
They make one vibrate well.
And sir, we are all vibrating.
All our bits of circles and cycles
Outside the Samsara in the ticks of
The time pieces in all our
Common chests. The basic kantan
Maxims make you do things like
Recalibrate and start joking around
Again. Run again. Feel again and
Write cutting poems everyday again.
Like you just may be continuing that
Morphology that sparked under a
Bamboo tree somewhere out...West?
East? Somewhere...It's like coming
Back was the wrong turn of phrase.
Because, as a student, you were always
There, always omnipresent like the
Meter you are frantically addicted
To. Because some books recommended
By good men, they can take you somewhere
Else and roll back the date. As if you
Were there outside time, everywhere,
Back home. Say it again because its
Persimmon sweet. Home.
In a city where nothing is wasted,
Not even a compliment.

Home. Where the wild purple flowers
Grow that opened up our eyes and sent
You back out to the world, a diplomat
Now of the hysterics involved in the
Middle way of our little heartland.
Home in the garden, with your mudra off
Center, but your spirit dilating all of known
History. Home, as you were just now.
Home. Home in Katano
Forever laughing too again.

What You Are Now

Are you this poem, friend?
Or perhaps the oak tree overlooking
The train tracks I have made my home?
Somewhere we know, all we are
Becomes something else. As we
Do not die I think.
From the curled up leash of this life
God hath bestowed with cruel limits.
Searching out one of us to cool
The benevolent cumulus, blanketing
Out the sun for a few moments,
Cooling the beggar's skin,
Safety is found in nature if searched out
If the will of the man is childish enough to find it.
As I eye the dancing Sunflower,
The summer ending now,
All seems to bow to time knowing
Well: the yellow petals sway here
Too, In tango with the sun the way they
Do under tomorrow's dawn,
Not concerned with
The clergy
Or laws
Of
Man.
Just the way you weren't
Concerned with god's decrees
Then.
Your whole life unfurling
Unwieldy and wild.

Waters in Your Tone

Under the fall moon.
Wide and heavy, the river.
It pounds at my spine,
As if to remind me
In your voice
All is relative
The way you said.
What that meant
Was you walking
The Earth too
Slow for I or
Anyone else
To comprehend.
Seeing Appalachia
And its breath or gawking
Up Jesus-high and Dionysus-drunk
At the Hollywood sign
Pointing to heaven.
That was enough
For you and I write these
Reminders to convince
Them. You were like
A magnetic storm becoming
The Auroras in the Arctic circle
A way point for the
Imagination. A figment of light
To guide the impossible.

In Response to the Season Change

And we mimic the seasons shivering
Hiding grudges against the wind and frightened
Like all the other animals. Though we may
Hold keys to migrate off the blue ball one day, we
Each night rest with eyes pointed straight up
Knowing even if the sun rises and riches
Wait, we are humbly subject to the royal cosmos.
As if at birth we entered a precarious time-
Line in which the debt we must pay for
Life amid our Goldilocks star were
Kneeling to fate and gods who claim to understand
Us all despite our great chasm of blindness
Under the matrix of stars which so
Confound us to the point of infinite maddening dissertations
From the womb to the grave. Yet the gods see
Our great foible and damn us to trickling
Amidst the falls of lives which seem on Ipod
Shuffle repeat until the end of all things.
Stars die, nations fall, lexicons evolve, languages
Are born, stones and bombs are cast about
From the whims of children and politicians and
That end reaches us all as seconds at a time
Visions of birth fade just the way all great baptisms
Evaporate in time. And that idea, falling from heaven
On arrival to Earth comes to signal
All codifications of god. Could it be?
Is it that heaven is a place not to ever be
Literally returned home to, but to be aspired
To in hope? In that infant-like sense of awe?

Tawagoto # 7

Sprinting Quasar amid
A dying, dancing religion and
Mother tongues rattling on the plains.
Summersaulting carbon burns
And sodomy flailing teen miscreants
Beneath puffy dawdling clouds
Who'd never know Newton or Jung or
Why Coitus opens a lottery to the universe.
Smuggling corn farmers
Bootlegging astronomers
Heretic Begonias and
Street-walking paperclips amid
The wrongfully accused Tao launderers.
I witness crimes reaching to the
Face of rebirth as though the
Soulless presidents deem the vagrants as devils and
Are shamelessly sprinting toward nirvana.
Sighting the folly of discerning man.
Copywriting criminology
Bigotry giraffes.
Deforestation Wichita Delano districts
It's all so confusing and the homeless
Zombified bum knows.
Graffiti spelunkers and
Resisting arrest Deacons.
They all seem so impermanent.
No?

A Humble Question

And the sun will rise
No matter how late you sleep
Or which god you see or pray to
And the vagrant will ask you,
Have you a song to play
Today, my friend?

Emerging Aspirant

For Shaune Larder

And my friend said like rain,
"Now as far from home as you
Ever will be it seems through
The tears and wakes,
Despite the storms which brew
In your stilting heart,
You've seen the young laugh
At war and dance in poverty.
So stop searching.
It's over now, my nervous
Student. You are becoming."

And to the womb I became.
Watching the teacher disappear
Off into the great horizon of time
On to the next lost student
I felt a great Baptism
Receding.
Never more frightened, I
Blinked and in that
One tenth second all I'd
Become to now
Fell into
View.

Before time I'd become the aether
Before the clamor of a singularity
Snapped all the galactic clusters into
Revolution
I, a ghastly nothing, neither
Fire nor air, not water, not soil,
Became the minute Planck
Lengths, the idea posterity and
Birth might never come, smaller
Than the absence of anything
At all. That was me:
A smudge, a precursory
Tinker-toy, a part of no matter,
No energy or alchemical
Spark. I'd become inertia.
Scattered in the infinitesimal so
That no light, dark, shadow
Or salvation would ever find me.
I became void. I became
Absence and all encompassing
Floating, tumbling, slithering waves
Of pure, quiet, blank and white noised
Silent, cosmological
Long-long ago.
I'd become the
Antiquity of all things.

Before the genesis of elements I
Snoozed about the pre-ejaculate of everything
That would burst into all we know. With

A pinching feeling, ignition was somehow
About to be achieved, that here and
There openings would arise into which
I and all we now know would be birthed
Unto and history could begin on
That cosmic array we know as real.

And the teacher was long gone off
Into the Oort cloud, among the comets
And the falling stars, knowing I would find
Him again, procrastinating his own
Mortality. I would arrive, singing in
Iambs, how I knew he'd given me
The peace of freedom yet isolated himself
Into the solidarity of teaching the universe
Nothing comes from anything with no force.
You create it.
Yourself.
And you taught it.
And I learned.
Becoming the student who sang of foolish professors.

From a Spartan

The trick is to walk somewhere
When you could have driven.
The trick is to stay cold and
Play with just how much thin air
You can get your lungs to breathe in.
Then run weightless come July.
The trick is to keep your head down
And keep your peripherals at attention
Looking dull, while being the most
Acutely aware man in the room,
In the whole town or
The whole country in this dark age
We don't know is devoid
Of light.
With this trick in certain moments, small
Micro-seconds, no one will know of but you,
Your brain will be the most enlightened
One.
On the whole planet.
That is if you take
Care and have the patience to
Spot it.

On a Friend's Life

I saw you fight between the reality of
Riding your bike seven miles to go wash
Dishes every day and singing to us
About how you really didn't want to
Flood your bloodstream with whiskey
And $3.49 Lo-Mein every night.
You wanted to be a human being,
Not a subscriber to this construct
We call society.
For you it didn't matter if a man had
Particularly nice paint brushes. It was
Just how he channeled his heart and
Mind through the bristles and back on
To the canvas. That message screamed
Into our ears and you stayed up
Till sunrise splattering it on your walls
So anyone who came to visit you
Would know: If you could free yourself
From the obligatory nature of this life,
Then maybe with an old beat up guitar
Simple people like us could do
Something for the world sitting in the
Gutter strumming as if our next
Meal depended upon it. And it has.
You were hungry. Your eyes had big red
Cracks. You didn't sleep. You filled your
Notebooks fat and it killed you.
But you were
Right here still.

Jackasses

We hit puberty strolling
To Seven-Eleven high
On weed we bought with nickels.
It was all the money we
Had. And we'd just smoked bay leaves
Mixed with oregano, dumb
Stoned on naive miscreance,
Hope, Ritalin, Black Sabbath
And rage. You didn't survive
It. I did. Your parents sobbed
As my third eye opened wide.
Thing was we didn't need leaves,
Powders, libations, needles
And paint thinner to see what
The world was trying to show
Us. We just had to freeze to
Death here and there a few times,
Cheat the reaping man, that scythe
Grazing our cheeks, hallucinate
Out of hunger and know rape
Well. These are good for artwork
And making the priest in the
Wooden box sob as we are lost
With our little stories and blood
Shot eyes. We knew the crowd said sleep,
And put a coat on man, can't
You see it's freezing? People are rocking in their seats
For you. For us and this line is written in red.
Your hallucinations have become real.

Taking up Residence

I started moving into Heaven
The first time I played guitar drunk
On vodka and tang. That night I knew
These drinks were called spirits for
Good reason and why shunned art
Types adored these altered states so much.
They took away mama yelling at dinner
And her pleads to, "Stop dancin', son, the
World will lock you up and throw away
The key for that kind of shit. Don't you
Know better? Now take your Clonazepam
And be quiet". The liquor took her voice right away.
It took away fathers dying and friends departing.
It took away fearing bombs fall from the sky
And world wars breaking out.
Knocking back this poison made me grow
In contradiction to myself, that sense every morning
Of my blood sugar on fire and the shakes, the
Shame and knowing the colonists had invented
This to destroy me and knowing I am still
Singing at the dinner table and a child. Still
Interpreting genesis the way I see it fit to,
Jotting notes from the Thesaurus just to break even
With my skewed cognition and word lust, just
So I know, no term you use
Will ever really demonize what I am,
My friend.

And the music makes all
Of these letters jingle with
That power and a sense of understanding.
I may know this house of blurred vision and
Euphoria well and it has become my home
Versificating amid the furious calls to
Cease all melodic efforts from doctors and
Law men in their terrified blindness.
It is in this state that I remain. Perhaps I am
Forever inebriated, mid waltz, paralyzed with rage in front
 of St. Peter.

Me Ignoring Doctors and Priests Again

You sip wine from a crystal
Glass while I gulp this piss beer,
An obtuse rotund
Brute and yet amid my storms
Each fall, ma'am you are there.
Time oozing forth, bloat
Of too many gods, fat words
And far too much cheap Moo Goo Gai Pan
Tell me I should have listened
When an east Asian monk friend told
Me, "Entropy comes and
Now you must go".
Basho playing harmonica in my mind as
Tom Petty fidgets with Koto
Harp strings and curiosity fosters
What the wind sounds like rustling
Between two Zen monks who keep trying
To get me to listen and stop jumping out of
Metaphorical windows and fleeing the real and
To stop being in a constant state of flagrant migration
From life to something more philosophical
And fairytale.
Then I sit, never minding it all,
Embracing the Zazen and disappearing
Into the black hills
Forever today.

A Birthday in Seoul

If I had one more
Song. Yeah, just one more
would do It. I'd say:

Look up.
Look up,

For what direction
Is that exactly anyway? Where
Is up when you've reached
The bottom of the Earth
And up still seems a
Bit further south?

I'd still shout, a grinnin'

Look up.
Look up, my friend.

I'll be there soon in
Terms of atomic decay,
You too shortly thereafter.
We've just to ferment
With the planet
For a few hundred million short
Years and to live on as
Cock rings, trash compactors,

Colostomy bags and all else
First. Yeah, that'll be us for
A little while, praying
To each of the gods,
For there are
Millions of them
Up
There.

Look up.
Look up and
See where it is we come from
And know one day we will go
There. Back home again.

Look up
Never at silly, fat Romans
Telling you where to
Set your eyes.

Look up

While most of your brothers live
And die with their blank faces
Pointed at their shoes.

Look up

And keep in mind,
The men who created Zeus

The men who thought up Buddha
The men who conceived Jesus,
They all looked up there
Too and scribbled as
Maniacs tend to
Do in the moments after
Setting truly open eyes
On the divine
With the nerve to ask how
It is we are here at all.

Look up
For all your years of
Hunching over.

Look up
At the pigeons and recall
Ms. Allen in 10th grade biology
Informing you, the little bird
Is just a distant cousin
To the pterosaurs that
Used to flap around
Up there.

Look up, you!
You, bloomed out of your
Mama's bulb and vines
Just as Kublai Khan was
And all the rest! This
Is birth! Above you!

Look up!

Because three messengers
Carried news of god once with no
Other hope in hell, but to spot
Hoshi dancers, hapless on
The way to a little town
Near Jerusalem.
No astrolabe, no sextant
No Tom-Tom, no crinkled atlas,
No Galaxy S8.
Just stars to lead them to
Witness Mary Magdalene's
Parthenogenesis
They had heard so much of.

Look up, darling.
Look up.
Where else do
You think Heaven has
Been this whole time?

Look up, you.
You and your ego!
Look up,

Noting the storm clouds drifting
On never seem to fear
The ride, so you shouldn't
Either.

Look up
Because comets may hurdle
Down from there
Sometimes to end you and all
Humankind's toys. But,
There are truths in promises
Of rapture.

Look up.
Right this moment,
Look up.
And you'll see if
You stare hard enough,
Everyone you've lost
Up until now.
They will live there someday
Or look there now at Orion's
Belt each night, Just as
You do.

Look up.
Not at fingers pointing there.

Just look up, straight up
At Polaris there.
You'll see the other red and blue
Shifting satellites turn wild as the world
Below Writhes revolving,
Flipping its poles. But,
Polaris? It'll just gawk back

Never moving, unphased,
At rest, fair, a friend,
Muted, without bias.
Remember. Straight up, still
As Polaris.
For as deities look down
At us, what is our duty
But to Spy upward proud
And defiant?
Polaris.
Polaris, friends.

Look up.
Look up,
Searching out the light
Millions of street
Lamps and neon liquor
Adverts tried to snuff out.

Look up
As you did then,
A child, curious
Wise and absent
Any fear at
All.

Look up
Because you won't be
Aspiring to your
Fellow man for too
Much longer.

Look up
Because celestial bodies
Seem to live beyond
The needs of coitus,
That anguish and
Detonation.

Look up
For a tick.
Look up.

There are no clocks.
No watches, no hour glasses to
Limit you among the dust
Greece so revered.
No dictums within it
Only decayed light
To tell you all of life's
Explosions
Cycle back. The thermonuclear
Winter always ends given
Patience.

Look up
Because death up
Skyward jigs about in tandem
With us, never quite demanding
End to the organic,
Just issuing time tables
As to when the elements

Are permitted to give life
From the aether.

Look up.
Look up!
Why?
Because the sun sits
Further up than any of the stain
Glass St. Peters with painted
Solar
Orbs behind them at mass
On Sunday. Those are symbols.
What's up there, my friend,
Is the face of god mankind
Forgot how to see.

Eyes up now, love.

We haven't years anymore,
Just a minute or two.
No time here for hands
In your pockets or glazed
Over eyes.
Point up to Betelgeuse.
Point to Canis Major.
And count them.
One gold and dying.
Two fat purple, gigantic as Rome
Was then. Only Parallax
Should have told Julius Caesar

That gods and empires are
Only vast from a certain
Point of view.

For good measure count them

One.   Two
One.   Two.
One.   Two.

Consider it this way.
The mathematics of it.
For to be clear, note,
There are more little bastard
Fractions between two integers,
Stars, whatever you want to
Call them, than in the whole
God damned
Number line.

Emperors	—	Tramps
Titans	—	Slaves
Kings	—	Mutts
Presidents	—	Holey pocketed bards
Tycoons —	Panhandlers	
Alpha	///	Omega
Diamonds	///	Carbon

    The wrinkled prong   —
The expecting womb

And again know
This.

Number one:

It's only gravity forces
Us here, to the dirt, to the
Grave, to fall back to all that magma
And nickel hell we rely on
Radio waves to tell us exists.
Fascist gravitational waves will
Pull me into nothing but
Silica bits, charging
Up the magnetosphere.
Like my body is lead gasoline
And the world a big old
Hummer to drive.
But no, I say.
I've more falling to do.
Much more.
Got to fall into Venus and
Got to fall into Mercury,
Through the sun too till it rains
Fire out past the Voyager probes
And
The planets are whisking
Round in the
Gogol-Atom bomb de-accretion
Disk cookie dough bowl
That
Used to be the solar system as
Time becomes something not so
Linear anymore and

The past becomes the
Future.
Through all that
I'll fall, drifting until
All descent becomes what
I've been looking for:

Home.
Just home and my black lab,
Even entropy having fallen apart.
My eyes crazed, happy and
Maniacal again.
Giddy for whatever infinity may
Become next.

And two:

Look there.
I haven't forgotten you yet.
You are crazy to think such
A thing even out here past the
Bounds of time.

Look up.
That is still what all of this
Is about.

And ask yourself again
In the mirror of Big Hole
River waters.

Do prattling, starved bluesmen
Whose souls depend
On the dark chocolate almond
Flavor of your lips,
Ever die at all? Do we really pass away?
Or do we simply become something else?
And that word.
Becoming,
Was that what all of this
Reckoning was about?
Could be.

Then,

Sit Indian style
Under a cherry blossom tree
When Persimmon season is
Just beginning and pray on
This.

He, me, I, him,
Whatever this is, has long
Since been removed.

But, he is still curious
Where and How much further south
He will have to go
To spot another Big Bang and
Catch you there
Again.

What Saved Me

A street waddling liquor sick Indian
Man I think might have tried to lead
Me back to god this afternoon. He told me, "Son, for
Us no mayors are going to speak up. No cop
Gonna give us any fry bread as
We panhandle downtown in the middle
Of winter. We are just going to walk
In this cold and shiver, waiting for
The sun to roll back for spring." And
Then I understood. This was our god, the sun.
Heat, warmth, the disc that seems to
Insist upon following us around all day up in the sky
And to trail off for the cold months to
Heat the others down south for a while.
Still though, I knelt for Mary these days,
Knew the Bodhisattvas were smarter than I,
That my Jew friend had peace, no guilt
That my classmate was a Brahmin and divine
Too. My Malawian buddy knew Christ was saving us
And Me, I just kept waiting in the cold. Waiting,
Drunk on promises of salvation.
A Maniac smile widening across
My face as the weather became more frigid.

Your Performance

For Michael Cissell

Shouting in the streets
Songs of yours this evening
My friend, in certain moments
I think I reached my hand in
To the porcelain cookie jar that holds
All the space between dead
Men and live ones. So my friend,
My friend that taught me sick love makes
The real work, our art, feasible,
My friend who lived just long enough
To dedicate a book of verse to his wife and sons.
My friend who refused to eat potatoes
Because carbohydrates are morally unsound
And in the same meal swigged quadruple
Wild Turkeys.
My friend, my teacher,
I sang your words tonight
Which I think made me you for a short time.
And so in front of the crowd
You were resurrected, my eyes shut,
Face and fingers numb, I read to
The people the eulogy you wrote
For yourself. Maybe it's that each
Line my pencil etches from here on
Out is something you play a small part
In. Knowing bards just may
Have no practical use for the
Hilarious concept of death.

To Be Anything

Seems some men born under the sun
Were told just to be lineman on the
Highschool football team, and sweaty cops,
Kneeling to the cross on Sunday, Inert.
To marry the first busty monosyllabic dish he met.
To accept that freedom happens two nights a week.
To become a numbed fungo bat eight hour unpaid lunch man.
To lease a beamer, because that! That is social currency!
To look down when the sun is in his eyes.
To forget the joy of being deathly sick, ditching school.
To leave youth behind and all that entails. All the running
 away and the rums and cokes.
To vote in all aspects, with dollar bills, and never his heart.
To listen to the same Katy Swift Montana Machine
Gun pop rock records on repeat again and again and more.
To unlearn the inherent creativity of digging a big
Fucking hole with a haggard stick or a Tonka truck in
The front yard under an oak tree on a hundred-degree day,
No parental guidance in sight.
To stare, a dullard, at the same TV reruns year after year.
To draw blinds shut come sunset, missing us all run west.
To work each day for internet and Roku
And Amazon insta-shop, Door dash and Cellophane
Wrapped Yaki-Soba over Piers Morgan Tonight
To procreate himself a boy with a biblical name so as
To join the obeisant Timothys and Josephs at confession
To obey the next war always comes, hydrogen bombs

Grow on, that tomorrow a sniping man
Will need to blow a combatant away
From a distance of ten football fields instead of
Nine, all to protect the quarterbacks at home.
To neglect waxing dreams after sex and Camel wides.
To exist as a spare part, a nut, a washer, a zip tie, a gob of glue
Instead of the vital impetus you are.
For every man wails in his stomach. It's just the
Pragmatic monochrome world tells him
Not to.
To tell the kiddos Jesus rose when he knows,
Like a toothache, the lord was just a man
Butchered, like all the far too righteous.
To introspect on the neighbor nanny, this envy man.
To divorce emotionally in a year, this fifty-year marrying man.
To rot his gut in trademarked aspartame, this commercial
    man.
To check the time always, refusing to exist outside the
Totalitarianism of clocks and calendars.
To acquiesce to his first-grade teacher who
Scolded him, told him he was a dummy,
Always would be too. And then,
And then someone tells him, "Son, that shit is wrong!"
And this man, half his life gone, is now born.

Hoping You Will Hear

Each evening when work is done
I cross my legs for Zazen and meditate
Just the way you taught me back then.
And the hoof beats coming from
My chest tell me, you can hear them
Too. In my heart the gales
Quiet down. The rain stops in my mind. I
Can hear the Shoji doors clatter open. And
Though the Earth lies between us I can feel you
Here. Then there you are sitting just
Like me. We smile for a moment,
Knowing what all our meals and prayers had
Been for in my past life, miss.
They were for this single moment remembering.

Matt Cooper is an English and creative writing major at Wichita State University. He has written and contributed to the Butler Lantern, Butler County Times-Gazette, and the WSU Sunflower newspapers as well as written poems that appeared in the *Mikrokosmos* literary journal. While pursuing a masters degree in poetry, Cooper has studied the Japanese language and literature at great length. He hopes to one day take residence in Katano, Osaka, Japan.